EYEWITNESS
BOY SCOUTS
OF AMERICA®

EYEWITNESS
BOY SCOUTS OF AMERICA®

Written by
ROBERT BIRKBY

DK

LONDON, NEW YORK,
MELBOURNE, MUNICH, AND DELHI

Senior editor Ros Walford
Senior art editor Ann Cannings
Production editor Kavita Varma
Senior production controller Verity Powell
Proofreader Eric Titner
Indexer Hilary Bird
Associate publisher Nigel Duffield

First published in the United States in 2012
by DK Publishing, 375 Hudson Street, New York, New York 10014

10 9 8 7 6 5 4 3 2 1
001–186414–Aug/12

Copyright © 2012 Dorling Kindersley Limited

DK books are available at special discounts
when purchased in bulk for sales promotions,
premiums, fundraising, or educational use.

For details, contact:
DK Publishing Special Markets
375 Hudson Street, New York, New York 10014
SpecialSales@dk.com

A catalog record for this book is available
from the Library of Congress.

ISBN 978-0-7566-9770-9

Color reproduction by Media Development & Printing Ltd., U.K.

Printed in China by Toppan Printing Co., Ltd.

Discover more at
www.dk.com

Pocketknife

Scout salute   Webelos badge

Boy Scouts of America®

The mission of the Boy Scouts of America is to prepare young people to make ethical and moral choices over their lifetimes by instilling in them the values of the Scout Oath and Law.

The programs of the Boy Scouts of America, Cub Scouting, Boy Scouting, Varsity Scouting, and Venturing, pursue these aims through methods designed for the age and maturity of the program participants.

Cub Scouting: A family- and home-centered program for boys in the first through fifth grade (or 7, 8, 9, and 10 years old). Cub Scouting's emphasis is on quality programs at the local level, where most boys and families are involved. Fourth- and fifth-grade (or 10-year-old) boys are called Webelos (WE'll BE LOyal Scouts) and participate in more advanced activities that begin to prepare them to become Boy Scouts.

Boy Scouting: A program for boys 11 through 17, designed to achieve the aims of Scouting through a vigorous outdoor program and peer group leadership with the counsel of an adult Scoutmaster. (Boys also may become Boy Scouts if they have earned the Arrow of Light Award or have completed the fifth grade).

Varsity Scouting: An active, exciting program for young men 14 through 17, built around five program fields of emphasis: advancement, high adventure, personal development, service, and special programs and events.

Venturing: Venturing is for young men and young women ages 14 through 20. It includes challenging, high-adventure activities, sports, and hobbies for teenagers that teach them leadership skills, provide opportunities to teach others, and give them an opportunity to learn and grow in a supportive, caring, and fun environment.

For more information on Scouting programs,
visit **www.scouting.org.**

Contents

Detail from
You can do it
by Joseph Csatari

What is Scouting?

THE BOY SCOUTS OF AMERICA is all about adventure. It's full of friendships, too, and opportunities to learn. Boys ages 7–10 join a Cub Scout pack. Boy Scouts are 11–18 years old, while Venturers are boys and girls ages 14–20. Each program is just right for its age group. Adult leaders help all Scouts succeed. For plenty of challenge and excitement, Scouting is the way to go.

Fun

Scouting is fun. There is plenty of opportunity to spend time outdoors. Scouts can go hiking, rock climbing, or do other exciting activities. They can camp out overnight and cook their meals over a campfire. Scouts plan their own activities and then figure out how to turn plans into action.

Service

All Scouts promise to do a Good Turn each day. An act of kindness could be carrying groceries for someone or asking a younger brother or sister to join in a game. Groups of Scouts can plan bigger projects, too. Repairing a hiking trail, painting a classroom, and cleaning up a park are all ways to help others.

Friendship

Scouting is a good way to make friends. Teamwork is important, and there are many times when Scouts depend on each other to get things done. They share adventures, too, and cheer each other on. Boys who get to know each other as Scouts might be friends for the rest of their lives.

Achievement

Scouts who complete requirements are given awards. They sew cloth patches onto their shirts to show everyone what they have done. The highest rank for Boy Scouts is Eagle. The Eagle Scout Award is a silver eagle hanging from a red, white, and blue ribbon.

Learning

While they are enjoying all they can do as Scouts, boys are also learning. They practice what to do in case of an emergency. They tie knots and figure out how to set up tents. Sometimes they meet Scouts from other places and hear about another part of the world.

Adventure

Scouting programs offer great outdoor adventures. Scouts can learn about wildlife and the environment. As they gain experience, they can go on more challenging trips. Scouting skills help everyone enjoy the outdoors safely. Scouts also learn how to protect the land.

Scouting begins

MORE THAN A CENTURY AGO, there were not many clubs for boys that would take them on outdoor adventures. A man in the United Kingdom named Robert Baden-Powell believed that if boys learned skills, such as survival and woodcraft, they would become more independent. He had an idea for an organization for boys that would be full of fun and excitement. He called it the Boy Scouts. As boys in the U.K. and other countries heard about it, they wanted to join. In 1907, the Scouting movement was born.

Mafeking

Robert Baden-Powell was an officer in the British army. He fought in the Boer War in South Africa (1899–1902). During this war, his soldiers were surrounded by the enemy in a town called Mafeking. He depended on local boys in a cadet corps to deliver messages. They helped to defend the town for 217 days. When more British soldiers freed the town, Baden-Powell and the cadets discovered they were famous.

Broad-brimmed army hat

Robert Baden-Powell

Baden-Powell wrote a book called *Aids to Scouting* to teach army Scouts how to live in the outdoors, travel without being seen, and report what they saw. When he learned that British boys were buying the book to try out the skills, he knew that the Boy Scouts would be a popular organization.

Military honors

Army uniform

Campfire sketch

Drawing was one of Baden-Powell's favorite hobbies. He made many sketches of Boy Scouts in action, including this one of boys relaxing around a campfire. The uniforms of the first Scouts looked like the clothing of Baden-Powell's cadet corps at Mafeking. The wide brims of their hats protected them from sun and rain.

Part I.

Price 4d. net

SCOUTING FOR BOYS BY B-P

LIEUT. GEN. BADEN POWELL C.B.

PUBLISHED BY HORACE COX, WINDSOR HOUSE, BREAM'S BUILDINGS, LONDON E.C.

The first Scouting book

Scouting for Boys was a book by Baden-Powell that showed boys how to be Scouts. It explained that at the heart of Scouting were patrols made up of six to eight boys working together. He asked boys to guide their lives by following Scout Law. It was based on the honor codes of knights from long ago. He also urged Scouts to "Do A Good Turn Daily" by being of service to other people.

Early New York Cub Scout pack

Cub Scouts

Cub Scouting began in the United Kingdom for boys who weren't old enough to be Boy Scouts. Stories from *The Jungle Book* by Rudyard Kipling brought "The Law of the Pack" and "Akela" to Cubs. Cub Scouts joined the Boy Scouts of America in 1930. Today, they enjoy a program with a wide variety of interesting activities. Cub Scouts have the encouragement of their families and neighborhoods.

America's first Scouts

THE BOY SCOUTS OF AMERICA was started in 1910 by a group of men who wanted boys to learn and grow. Some of Scouting's founders had experimented with youth groups of their own. They mixed their ideas with those of Robert Baden-Powell's British Scouts. The result was an organization full of excitement and adventure. Three of the first American Scout leaders were Ernest Thompson Seton, Daniel Carter Beard, and James E. West.

Native American values

Before Scouting began, Ernest Thompson Seton led the League of Woodcraft Indians (renamed the Woodcraft League of America), an organization for young people that honored the values of Native Americans. Seton's book, *The Birch Bark Roll*, explained how boys could camp out using Native American traditions. They could also study wildlife, learn skills, and earn awards.

Ernest Thompson Seton

When he was a boy, Ernest Thompson Seton liked to walk in the woods and watch birds, deer, and other wildlife. He became a famous artist and wrote books about animals. Seton wanted young people to enjoy hiking and camping, too. He brought his love of wildlife to the BSA and taught Scouts about being in the outdoors.

Lobo

Lobo was a wolf living in the mountains of New Mexico. Ernest Thompson Seton admired Lobo so much that he began calling himself Black Wolf and drew a wolf footprint next to his signature. He wrote stories about Lobo as the strong leader of a wolf pack and painted this picture of him. Today, one of the ranks that Cub Scouts can earn is Wolf.

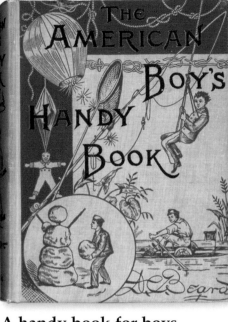

A handy book for boys

In *The American Boy's Handy Book,* Daniel Carter Beard shared dozens of projects he knew boys would like. There were patterns for building kites and canoes, and instructions for shooting a bow and arrow. Many of his plans appeared later in books for Scouts.

Daniel Carter Beard

"Uncle Dan" Beard often wore the leather clothing of the frontier. Like Seton, he had started his own group for boys. They were called the Sons of Daniel Boone. Members learned to use axes, knives, and their hands to build log cabins and other projects in the forest. Daniel Beard brought those outdoor skills to Scouting.

James E. West

James E. West's parents died when he was a child. A disease crippled his leg. He did his best to face those challenges. He worked his way through college and became a lawyer. As Chief Executive of the Boy Scouts for more than 30 years, West led the BSA as it grew into a strong national organization with millions of members.

Boy Scout uniforms

WHEN BOYS WEAR A UNIFORM to play soccer or baseball, they know that they are part of a team. That's why the Scouts wear uniforms, too. It helps them to know that they belong and are equal. When people see boys wearing Scout uniforms, they know that they can be trusted to do the right thing. The Boy Scouts of America uniform has changed over the years. Each change has made the uniform better for its time. Even so, Scouts from any year still looked like Scouts.

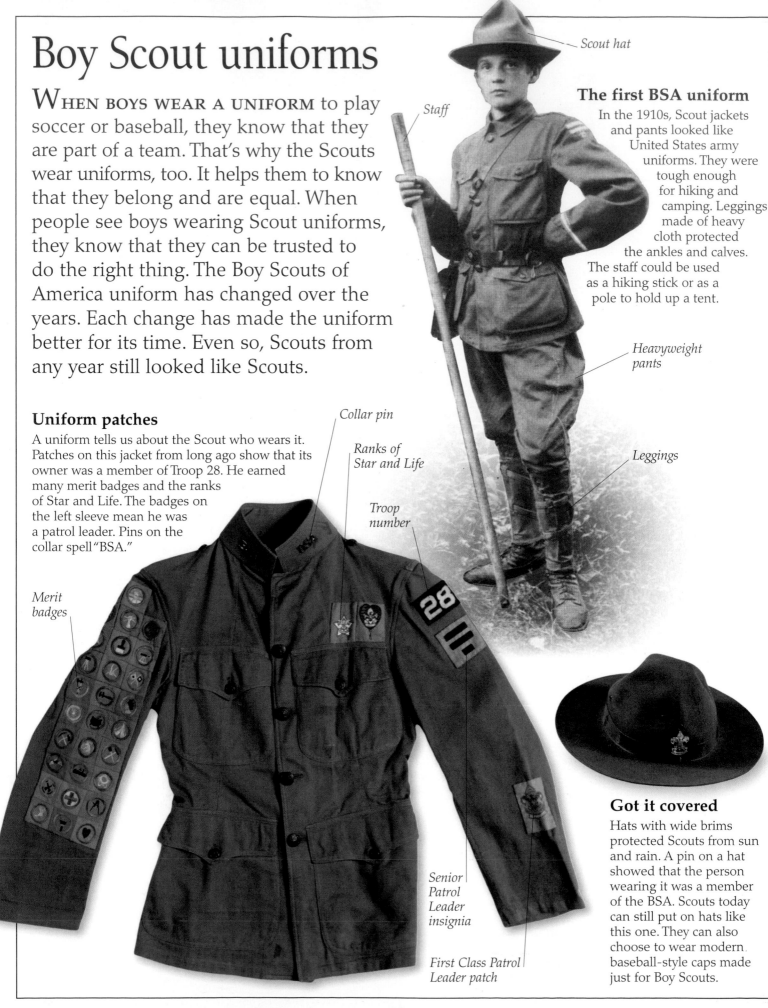

Scout hat

Staff

The first BSA uniform
In the 1910s, Scout jackets and pants looked like United States army uniforms. They were tough enough for hiking and camping. Leggings made of heavy cloth protected the ankles and calves. The staff could be used as a hiking stick or as a pole to hold up a tent.

Heavyweight pants

Leggings

Uniform patches
A uniform tells us about the Scout who wears it. Patches on this jacket from long ago show that its owner was a member of Troop 28. He earned many merit badges and the ranks of Star and Life. The badges on the left sleeve mean he was a patrol leader. Pins on the collar spell "BSA."

Collar pin

Ranks of Star and Life

Troop number

Merit badges

Senior Patrol Leader insignia

First Class Patrol Leader patch

Got it covered
Hats with wide brims protected Scouts from sun and rain. A pin on a hat showed that the person wearing it was a member of the BSA. Scouts today can still put on hats like this one. They can also choose to wear modern baseball-style caps made just for Boy Scouts.

Scout Cap

Neckerchief

Neckerchief slide

Red trim on pocket

Gaiters

1950s uniform

By the 1950s, Scout shirts and pants were a color called olive green. Pants pockets had red trim. Gaiters were worn to keep pebbles and snow out of hiking boots. When a Scout wasn't wearing his cap, he could fold it over his belt. Many Scouts still carried a wooden staff.

High Adventure Base neckerchief

Neckerchiefs

A neckerchief is held in place with a neckerchief slide. All members of a troop wear neckerchiefs of the same color. A Scout can use his neckerchief to bandage a wound or to make a sling for a hurt arm. He can also use it to keep dust out of his nose and mouth.

BSA standard-issue slide

Homemade slide

Modern uniform

Today's Boy Scout uniform is made for action. It looks great for troop meetings and public events. There is plenty of room in the cargo pockets to carry belongings. Patches that show troop number and rank can be sewn onto the shirt. The uniform even has socks—green with a red band around the top.

Scout adventures

SCOUTS LOVE ADVENTURES. Today, they ride mountain bikes and paddle kayaks and canoes. They climb mountains and rappel on ropes to get back down. In the early days of Scouting, boys set off on adventures, too. They liked to hike and camp as much as modern Scouts do. Some of their equipment was different though. Here are some of the items that early Scouts would have carried with them.

Leather straps and metal buckles

Rings for lashing items to the pack

Trapper Nelson pack

A pack holds the equipment a Scout will need while he is hiking and camping. This early pack was designed by a man named Lloyd Nelson. It became a favorite with Scouts. Its wooden frame helped to balance the weight on the Scout's shoulders. A flap closing the top protected the gear inside from rain and snow.

Heavy cloth bag

Wooden pack board

Pocketknife

A pocketknife is a Scout's most useful tool. It has not changed very much in the past 100 years of Scouting. Most pocketknives have one or two blades for cutting. They also have a screwdriver, a can opener, and a bottle opener. The decoration on this old knife shows Scouts around a campfire.

Bottle opener and screwdriver

Can opener

The first camp—Silver Bay, 1910

Soon after the Boy Scouts of America started, boys from Boston camped at Silver Bay on the shore of Lake George in New York State. They slept in big canvas tents and cooked their meals over an open fire. They did not have uniforms, but they had plenty of fun and adventure.

Antiseptic

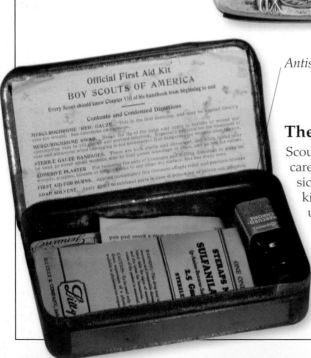

The first BSA first aid kit

Scouts have always learned how to care for someone who is hurt or sick. The first official BSA first aid kit held supplies that could be used in an emergency. There was antiseptic for killing germs. Bandages were for stopping bleeding and keeping cuts clean. A small book in each first aid kit gave instructions on what to do for many illnesses and injuries.

Scout whistle

Scouts who get lost should S.T.O.P! That means Stop, Think, Observe, and Plan. Blowing on a whistle is a good way to attract the attention of people who can come and help. In the early days, Scouts would have used a metal whistle like this one.

Hikemeter

Scouts in the 1930s could use this hikemeter to tell them how far they had walked. A compass on the back of the hikemeter showed them which way to go. These days, a Scout might get the same kind of information by using an application on a cell phone.

Numbers show total distance

Hands move with each step

Scout ax

Knowing how to use an ax was an important Scouting skill. On outdoor adventures, they used the ax to chop trees for firewood and shelters. Many Scouts still learn how to swing an ax, but today they usually leave it at home when they go on expeditions. They carry lightweight stoves and tents instead.

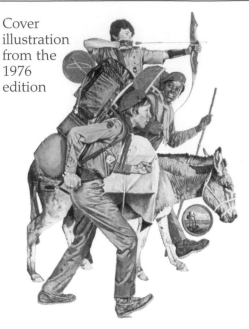

Cover illustration from the 1976 edition

The Boy Scout Handbook

A BOOK CALLED *The Boy Scout Handbook* explains all about Boy Scouting. The first copy was printed more than 100 years ago. It used to be called *Handbook for Boys*. A new edition is written every 10 years or so. This is because the world changes and the Boy Scouts of America needs to keep up. For example, the first handbook had a badge for poultry farming. The newest version includes a badge for computer science.

Pages from the first edition

First edition, 1911

The 12 editions of *The Boy Scout Handbook* are different from each other, but the Scout Oath and Law have never changed. The Scout sign, salute, motto, and slogan are the same, too.

First edition cover

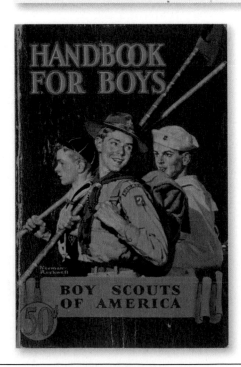

Second edition, 1914

This cover shows Scouts sending messages using flags. This is called semaphore. The flags are held in a different position for each letter. Before telephones, this was an important way to send emergency messages.

Fourth edition, 1940

Members of three BSA programs—Cub Scouts, Boy Scouts, and Sea Scouts—appear on the cover of the 1940 handbook. The Cub Scout and Boy Scout are wearing neckerchiefs and carrying hiking sticks on their shoulders.

Sixth edition, 1959

The Boy Scout Handbook has always been an exciting guide to outdoor adventures. This edition is full of colorful drawings of boys hiking, camping, swimming, and learning about wild animals.

YOU — IN THE GREAT OUTDOORS

When you are a Scout, forests and fields, rivers and lakes, are your playground. You are completely at home in God's great outdoors. You learn to notice every sound, to observe every track. Birds and animals become your friends. You master the skills of walking noiselessly through the woods, of stalking close to a grazing deer without being noticed, of bringing a bird to you by imitating its call. You learn to find your way cross country by map and compass, to make a meal when you are hungry, to take a safe swim when you are hot, to make yourself comfortable for the night in a tent or under the stars. You become a true outdoorsman.

Pages from the sixth edition

Eighth edition, 1972

Scout adventures happen everywhere. The 1972 handbook explained how boys in cities could enjoy Scouting without going very far from home. That was also true for boys from small towns.

SPECIAL-INTEREST HIKE

You can hike in the city or town. Your hike plan should cover the same points as your 5-mile hike in the field. What things of special interest are there where you live?

Museum
Zoo
Park
Factory
Art gallery
Historic site
Dairy
Cattle ranch
Sewage plant

Phone ahead to be sure that you can visit without an adult.

Birdseed.—Make this mixture yourself with the things you like. Put in dry, sugar-coated cereal, one small package of raisins, a half cup of unsalted peanuts or cashew nuts, and a small package of candy-coated chocolates. Enjoy a few handfuls when you are tired and hungry.

198

Pages from the eighth edition

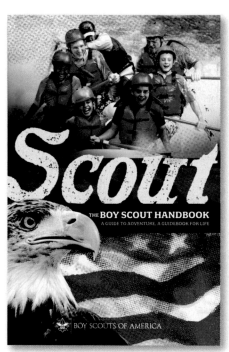

Twelfth edition, 2009

The newest handbook mixes excitement and learning with service and achievement. All the other handbooks have done that, too. Each was the right book for its time and for the readers who turned its pages.

Cub Scouts

Cub Scouting is a great adventure for boys who are in the first grade through the fifth grade (ages 7 through 10). It is full of exciting things to do. Hiking through a forest, cooking over a campfire, building projects, and doing good things for others are just a few Cub Scout activities. A Cub pack is made up of dens, each with six to eight boys. Together they travel, learn, play, and get things done.

Webelos

Webelos are Cub Scouts who are 10 years old and getting ready to join a Boy Scout troop at age 11. They can wear Boy Scout shirts and earn the Arrow of Light patch, the highest award in Cub Scouting.

Academics and sports programs

Cub Scouts learn about many subjects. They might try astronomy, chess, computers, and science. They can also have fun with sports including golf, hiking, tennis, skateboarding, and soccer.

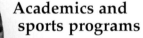

Advancement

By passing tests, Cub Scouts earn patches to sew onto their shirts. The big patches on this Scout's left pocket are for the four ranks of Cub Scouting: Tiger, Wolf, Bear, and Webelos. The gold and silver arrow points are steps on the way to earning ranks.

Friendship

Joining the Cub Scouts is a great way to make friends. When boys do things together, they have lots to share. Some boys who meet as Cub Scouts stay friends for years.

Teamwork

All Cub Scouts help whenever he can. They know that working together is important. That's true in tug-of-war and in everything else that Cub Scouts do. Parents and other family members often assist with events.

The Tiger Cub flag

Cub Scout visits

Many Cub Scout dens get to visit exciting places, such as a fire station. There, they might explore a fire truck or try on a firefighter's helmet. They might also visit a neighborhood police station or a television station to see how programs are made.

Tiger Cubs

The first rank a Cub Scout earns is Tiger Cub. To earn this rank, he has to finish 15 activities. He gets a colored bead for each activity. Like these boys, he can wear the beads on his Tiger Cub Totem. That's a tiger footprint buttoned to the right pocket of his uniform shirt.

Cub Scout meetings

CUB SCOUTING MEANS DOING THINGS. That starts with den meetings. Cub Scouts get together with each other to have fun and learn new skills. They can get ready for adventures that might include camping, hiking, racing model cars, going on field trips, and doing projects that help their hometowns and the people who live there. Meetings are also a time for Cub Scouts to think about the Scout values that help them become the best people they can be.

Den leaders

Each Cub Scout den has adult leaders. They can be the parents and guardians of Cub Scouts. "Akela" is a title given to any good leader. Akela is also the leader and guide for Cub Scouts on the Wolf trail. Many dens have a Den Chief, too. That's a Boy Scout who can teach skills and be a good role model.

Playing games

Scouting is a game with a purpose. Whether it's a balloon race, a tug-of-war, a few innings of softball, or an obstacle course, games are exciting ways for Cub Scouts to build their den into a strong team. Fair play and support for one another are important to Cub Scout games, too.

Cub Scout sign

Cub Scouts make the Cub Scout sign at meetings as they repeat the Cub Scout oath. That is a reminder of the values of Scouting. They can also salute the American flag and recite the Pledge of Allegiance. A den leader might have a story to tell or suggest a song that gives Cub Scouts something to think about after the meeting ends.

Building a project

Cub Scouts love to build things. A project might be a Pinewood Derby race car, a model sail boat, or a propeller-driven rocket that will fly along a line. They can also dive into projects that help their neighborhoods. That can mean planting trees, painting park benches, and collecting canned goods to take to community food banks.

Learning by doing

Cub Scouts get to decide what they want to do. They help plan what their den will do. Learning to share ideas is important, too. That way everybody has a chance to be heard. Each Cub Scout has a role to play in getting ready for den activities. As Cub Scouts gain experience, they can take part in bigger adventures

Pinewood Derby®

DREAM! BUILD! RACE! Those are the steps for the Pinewood Derby. It's one of the biggest events of the Cub Scout year. Start with a block of wood and a set of wheels. Imagine the kind of racer you want. A parent or other adult will help you build the car and enter it in your Cub Scout pack's Pinewood Derby. Win or lose, you'll be cheering your racer to be the best as it flies down the Pinewood Derby track.

Building your kit

Turning a block of wood into a racer is very rewarding. The official Pinewood Derby racer kit has the basic parts. Use a saw and sandpaper to shape the wood. Nails that come with the kit are the axles that hold the wheels in place.

Pinewood Derby blueprint

A blueprint, or template, helps you to design your car according to the Pinewood Derby rules. To be fair to all entrants, each racer can weigh no more than 5 ounces. The body of the car must be less than 7 inches long and 1¾ inches wide. The wheels on every racer are the same size, too. This car blueprint was printed in *Boys' Life* magazine in 1954.

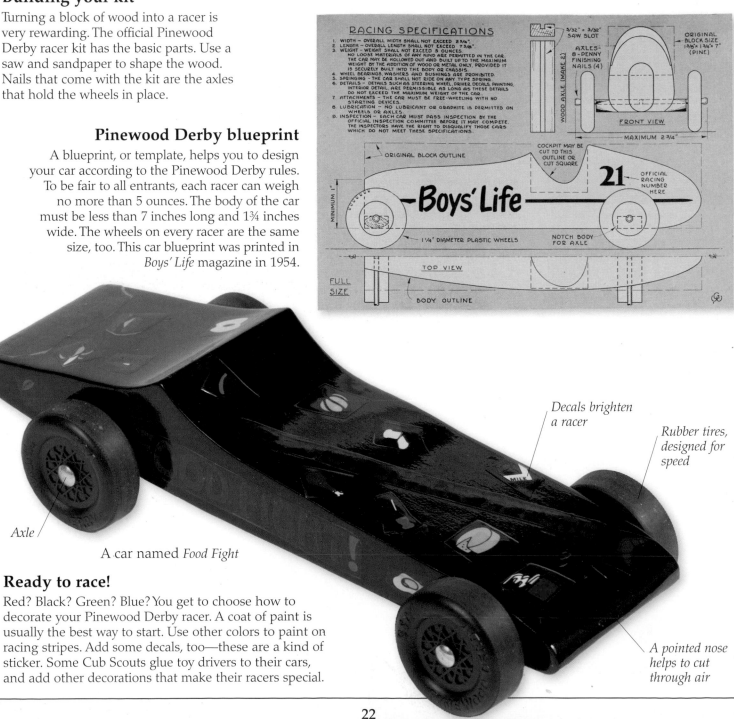

Ready to race!

Red? Black? Green? Blue? You get to choose how to decorate your Pinewood Derby racer. A coat of paint is usually the best way to start. Use other colors to paint on racing stripes. Add some decals, too—these are a kind of sticker. Some Cub Scouts glue toy drivers to their cars, and add other decorations that make their racers special.

Axle

A car named Food Fight

Decals brighten a racer

Rubber tires, designed for speed

A pointed nose helps to cut through air

One of a kind

Since the first Pinewood Derby race in 1953, Cub Scouts have built more than 100 million cars. Add up the distances all of them have traveled, and it's enough miles to go to the moon and back. Every car has been different, but they're all fast.

Cheering on the team

A Pinewood Derby lets Cub Scouts and adults work and learn together to complete their cars. That makes everyone a winner. The day of the Derby is a fun time for all Cub Scouts. Awards are given for the best decorated cars and for those that are the fastest. Your Pinewood Derby racer will become a reminder of good times.

A Pinewood Derby trophy

Scout values

Character counts by Joseph Csatari, 1995

THE OATH AND LAW are the rules of the Boy Scouts of America. They help Scouts make good choices in their lives. Being honest, friendly, and kind are three ways that Scouts act every day. They also learn about first aid, the outdoors, and citizenship. They know what to do in emergencies, and are brave enough to do the right thing even when friends might make wrong choices. The BSA gives boys the knowledge and experience to become leaders.

On my honor I will do my best
to do my duty to God and my country and to obey the Scout Law;
to help other people at all times;
to keep myself physically strong, mentally awake,
and morally straight.

Scout Oath

A Scout is
trustworthy, loyal, helpful,
friendly, courteous, kind,
obedient, cheerful, thrifty,
brave, clean, and reverent.

Scout Law

Scout sign

The three raised fingers of the Scout sign represent the three parts of the Scout Oath. When a leader raises the sign, Scouts know it is time to be quiet and pay attention. They also form the sign while reciting the Oath and Law.

Cub Scout values

The values of Cub Scouts are explained in the promise and motto that each Cub Scout learns to say. They give boys guidance for living good lives. The promise and motto lead to the bigger ideas of the Boy Scout Oath and Law. Cub Scouts who become Webelos learn the Boy Scout Oath and Law as they prepare to join a Boy Scout troop.

I, [name], promise to do my best
To do my duty to God and my country,
To help other people, and
To obey the Law of the Pack.

Cub Scout Promise

Do Your Best.

Cub Scout motto

The eagle and shield show a Scout's readiness to defend freedom

Two stars mean truth and knowledge

Living the values

The BSA asks Scouts to do their best to live according to the Oath and Law. Scout meetings and activities help them to reach that goal. Scouts can discover lots of ways to do the right thing. The values of Scouting can be important guides for their lives.

The Scout badge

Scouts proudly wear the badge of the BSA. It is shaped like the north point of a compass. Each part of the badge reminds Scouts of the values of the BSA.

The scroll holds the Scout motto

The knot represents the slogan "Do A Good Turn Daily"

A Good Turn daily

WHEN A BOY SCOUT DOES something to help others, it is called a Good Turn. It is so important that "Do A Good Turn Daily" has become the slogan of the Boy Scouts of America. Every Scout is expected to do at least one Good Turn every day without payment. Helpfulness is one of the qualities that people respect when they meet Boy Scouts.

The first Good Turn

In 1909, American businessman William Boyce was lost in the London fog. A boy helped him to find his way. Mr. Boyce offered to pay him, but the boy said, "I am a Scout and we don't take money for doing Good Turns." Mr. Boyce learned more about Scouting in the United Kingdom and brought the idea to the United States.

Helping others

Opening a door for someone is a Good Turn. Helping an older person clean her house might require some planning, but that is a Good Turn, too. Good Turns can be small or large. What really matters is that a Scout is making a difference.

Serving the community

Good Turns make communities better places to live. Picking up litter and shoveling snow from sidewalks are projects that help everyone. A Scout might offer to mow the lawn of an elderly neighbor or promise to deliver groceries. Good Turns can be fun to do, especially when Scouts who are friends work together for the benefit of others.

Caring for the environment

Many Scouts use Good Turns to care for the Earth. Planting trees, pulling weeds, and repairing hiking trails can be terrific projects. Building birdhouses and restoring streams are both good ways to help local wildlife. They improve the places where animals live.

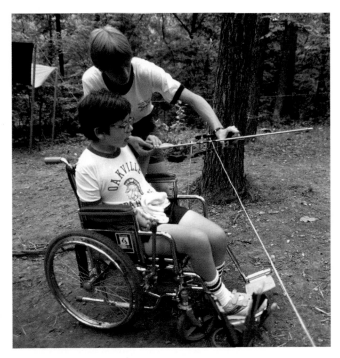

Acts of kindness

A Good Turn can be as simple as helping a friend to learn a new skill at camp. By doing Good Turns, a Scout gets into the habit of taking action whenever he sees the opportunity to help someone else.

National Good Turns

Each year, thousands of Boy Scouts volunteer to take part in a Good Turn called "Scouting for Food." They collect cans of food donated by their neighbors and then deliver the cans to food banks. It's a way of helping the homeless and other people in need to receive healthy meals.

Service to others

WHEN SCOUTS REPEAT THE OATH, they promise they will "help other people at all times." One way of doing this is to be prepared for emergencies. Another is to carry out projects that do something good for others or for the environment. Working next to friends can be fun, too. Scouts don't ask to be paid for helping out. The satisfaction of knowing they have done their best is enough of a reward.

Treasury medal

During World War I, some of the first Boy Scouts raised money to help the war effort. The United States thanked those Scouts by giving them special medals from the Treasury Department.

Helping the community

Scouts of all ages pitch in to make their neighborhoods better places to live. These young Scouts are planting trees in a park. That will make the area look better for years to come. It is also good for the environment.

Doing their part

Some thoughtless people paint letters and pictures on walls that are not their property. This graffiti is hard to remove. Some people leave trash on the ground, too. Scouts often get together to fix up their neighborhoods. Getting rid of litter and removing graffiti can really help to keep an area tidy. Recycling paper and cans helps, too.

Rivers and lakes

Mountains and forests

Ready to go

Helping to paint the home of an older person could be a good Saturday project for a pack of Cub Scouts. They might paint benches in a city park, too. Every little bit helps, and Scouts can help a lot.

Leave No Trace patch

Scouts follow the principles of Leave No Trace by leaving places better than when they found them. The LNT patch is awarded to recognize that Scouts have cared for the environment.

Digging in

A Cub Scout pack leader shows boys how to trim a flower bed to keep it healthy. The plants protect the soil from erosion. Seeing flowers often makes people feel happier. By planting flowers in a public place, the Scouts have done something good for the community.

The registration card you receive when you join shows that you are a member of the Boy Scouts of America.

Joining the troop

Boys who are 11 years old can join a Boy Scout troop. Boy who have finished 5th grade, or who are 10 years old and have earned the Cub Scout's Arrow of Light Award, can also join. They get membership cards of their own and will find a warm welcome from other Scouts.

Boy Scouts

A GROUP OF BOY SCOUTS is called a troop. Each troop is made up of patrols. Patrols are teams of six to eight boys. They often become great friends. In the winter they might build snow caves and spend the night. In the summer they do plenty of camping, hiking, swimming, and learning. As Scouts gain experience, they can plan bigger adventures. Many explore mountain trails, rivers, and forests.

Teaching new skills

Older Scouts teach skills to new troop members. When a younger boy has mastered a new skill, he can receive an award. For example, one test for earning the Second Class badge is lighting a fire. An older Scout shows how to build the campfire by arranging sticks in the shape of a tepee. Scouts also learn to use fire safely. Sometimes that means not building a fire at all.

Scoutmaster

Many adults support the troop. Parents and other family members lend a hand. The troop's most important adult is the Scoutmaster. One of his jobs is to teach Scouts to be good leaders. He lets an older Scout called the senior patrol leader have the main role at troop meetings. The Scoutmaster helps the senior patrol leader to succeed.

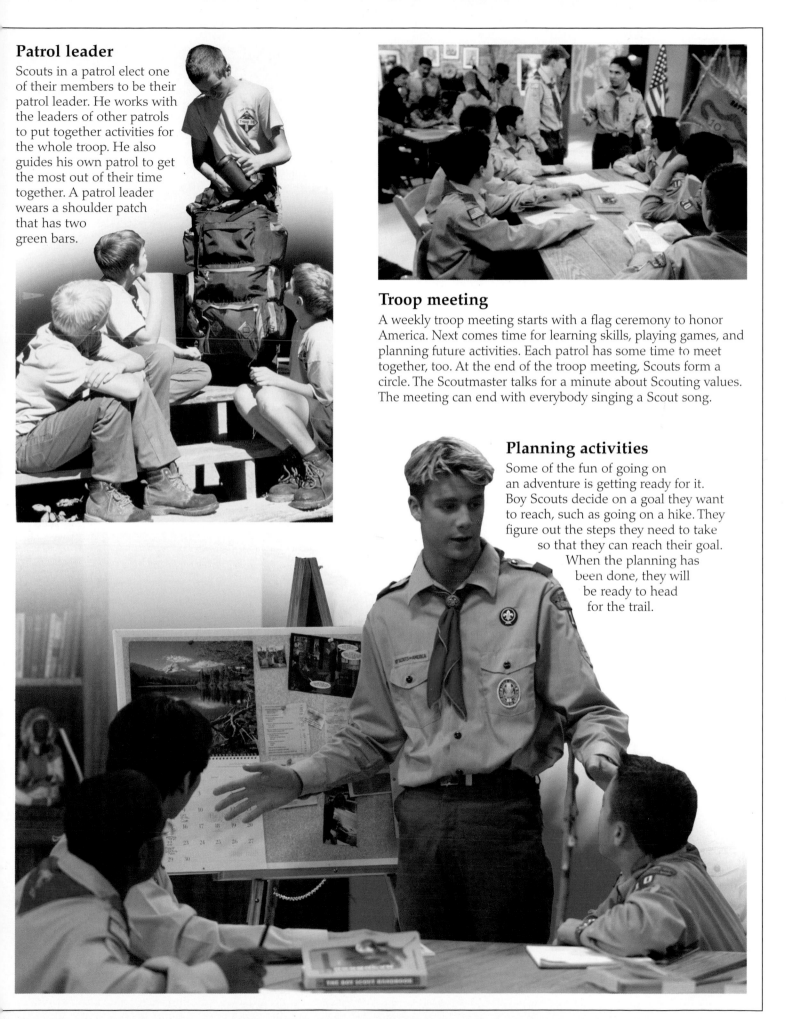

Patrol leader

Scouts in a patrol elect one of their members to be their patrol leader. He works with the leaders of other patrols to put together activities for the whole troop. He also guides his own patrol to get the most out of their time together. A patrol leader wears a shoulder patch that has two green bars.

Troop meeting

A weekly troop meeting starts with a flag ceremony to honor America. Next comes time for learning skills, playing games, and planning future activities. Each patrol has some time to meet together, too. At the end of the troop meeting, Scouts form a circle. The Scoutmaster talks for a minute about Scouting values. The meeting can end with everybody singing a Scout song.

Planning activities

Some of the fun of going on an adventure is getting ready for it. Boy Scouts decide on a goal they want to reach, such as going on a hike. They figure out the steps they need to take so that they can reach their goal. When the planning has been done, they will be ready to head for the trail.

Scouting activities

ACTION, EXCITEMENT, AND ADVENTURE are all part of Scouting. That's why many boys join a troop. They go hiking, camping, bicycling, and canoeing, and they find plenty of other ways to have fun. Outdoor activities prepare Cub Scouts, Boy Scouts, and Venturers for the challenges of life. Scouts with disabilities can take part in outdoor activities, too. Other Scouts encourage them to succeed.

Campout

Campouts are favorite events for Scouts. Scouts take food and equipment with them to a campsite. They usually choose a good spot, such as near a lake, by a meadow, or under some trees. There they set up tents and cook meals. Before crawling into their sleeping bags, the Scouts might sit around a campfire singing songs and telling stories.

Rappelling

Rappelling is a way to slide down a rope that is tied to the top of a cliff. A Scout wears a harness around his waist. The rope goes through a metal ring attached to the harness, and the Scout controls his speed by bending the rope against the ring. Doing it the right way is safe, satisfying, and thrilling.

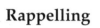

Cycling

A lot of Scouts enjoy cycling. Some pedal for many miles along quiet roads. Others use mountain bikes to take on steep trails. Riders on BMX bikes (bicycle motocross) wear knee pads for protection while on special obstacle courses. Many Scouts earn the Cycling merit badge.

Horseback riding

Many summer camps have stables of horses. Scouts learn how to care for horses by feeding them and brushing their coats. Once the saddle is on a horse, a Scout can step into the stirrup and take the reins. There is a lot of trust between a horse and a rider as they make their way down a trail.

Stargazing

The adventure of Scouting doesn't end at sunset. Boys looking up at the night sky see stars sparkling everywhere. Telescopes can give them close views of craters on the moon, the rings of Saturn, and the Milky Way. Scouts learn to identify the North Star and constellations including the Big Dipper and Orion.

Summer camp

Summer camp is a real highlight for every Scout. For a day or a week, Cub Scouts, Boy Scouts, and Venturers can sample archery ranges, trails, and swimming and boating activities. There is plenty of time to pass requirements for awards, too.

Fishing

Cub Scouts spend happy afternoons fishing lakes. All they need is a pole, a line, and a little patience. There are lots of other ways Scouts can learn about nature, too. They include watching birds, studying insects, and identifying plants.

Water sports

There's nothing better on a hot summer day than being out on the water. Scouts paddle kayaks and canoes on rivers and lakes. A pool at summer camp is just right for swimming. Many Scouts earn badges for swimming and lifesaving. There's a Mile Swim patch, too, for going the distance.

Hiking

Scouts love to explore, and trails will lead them to
great adventures. A short hike in a city park can be full
of things to see and do. Splashing through the mud is hard
to beat for a good time. Older Scouts fill their packs with
gear and food and set off on trips deep into the backcountry.
They camp at night and cook their meals over a stove or open fire.

Navigating

The needle on a compass always points north.
Using a map and compass together, Scouts find
their way even in places they've never
been to before. They can also work out
where they are with Global
Positioning System
(GPS) receivers that
bounce signals off
satellites.

High adventure

THE MORE THAT SCOUTS LEARN, the more they get to do. Older boys who have been on plenty of troop campouts are ready for bigger experiences. They can go on long backpacking trips, canoe for a week on wilderness lakes, and climb to the tops of mountains. Some sail ships. Others build igloos. They understand first aid, what to do in a storm, and how to find their way home. Put it all together, and it is Scouting high adventure.

Going high

With lumberjack spurs on his boots and a big belt around his waist, a Scout climbs a pole. This really is a high adventure. To keep every Scout safe, instructors teach boys the right way to do each activity.

Expeditions

On an expedition, Scouts go backpacking for several days or even weeks. They talk to each other while they walk. At rest stops, they drink from water bottles and eat snacks. By the end of the day they will reach a campsite, and the next morning wake up ready for another day on the trail.

Philmont

Philmont Scout Ranch is a national high adventure base in northern New Mexico. Scouts can backpack there for 10 days in mountains as high as 12,000 feet. As they are leaving Philmont, some Scouts toss worn out boots over the welcome gate. Other high adventure bases are at Northern Tier and the Florida Sea Base.

Northern Tier

Scouts at Northern Tier can take canoe trips deep into the wilderness of the Great North Woods of Minnesota and Canada. They paddle routes once traveled by French explorers and fur trappers. Some crews catch fish and cook them for dinner back at camp. There is plenty of wildlife to see, too, including birds, moose, and porcupines.

Florida Sea Base

Many Scouts pass tests to become SCUBA divers at the Florida Sea Base. With tanks of air on their backs, they can explore coral reefs and swim with schools of brightly colored fish. Sea Base Scouts can also set sail across the beautiful waters of the Florida Keys.

Venturing

YOUNG MEN AND WOMEN who want to have Scouting adventures become Venturers. They are between 14 and 20 years old. They plan terrific activities and then make them happen. Venturers also learn to be good leaders and work to improve their communities. For example, they might help children at a neighborhood school learn to read.

Rappelling

This exciting activity involves using ropes to descend from a tower, building, or cliff. Rappelling builds confidence in Venturers. Another Venturer controls safety ropes called belay lines to give rappellers extra protection.

Mountaineering

Trekking or climbing in the mountains is a fantastic adventure. Venturers carry all of their gear and food in a backpack. They might hike to a lake or to the summit of a high peak. Sometimes, they camp out under the stars. They use a map and compass to keep from getting lost.

Sea Scouts

Sea Scouts are Venturers who go out in boats or on ships. They learn how to take care of their ship and how to handle it on lakes or in the ocean. A voyage might last for days or just a few hours. Many Sea Scout ships have sails. By pulling on ropes to adjust the sails, Sea Scouts use the wind to push their ship forward.

Winter camping

When cold weather comes, Venturers still like to head outdoors. They put on warm clothing and carry everything they need on a sled. If it is cold enough, they can make camp on a frozen lake. They might use an auger to drill a hole through the ice and catch some fish.

Water sports

To explore underwater, many Venturers learn how to scuba dive. ("Scuba" stands for Self Contained Underwater Breathing Apparatus.) Divers breathe from oxygen tanks. Flippers on their feet add power as they swim. They might explore reefs full of colorful fish or even a shipwreck. Venturers also use canoes, kayaks, and rafts to explore rivers and lakes.

Basic essentials

SCOUTS CARRY 10 USEFUL ITEMS with them during outdoor adventures. These basic essentials keep them warm and dry in all kinds of weather. When Scouts aren't sure where to go, they have tools to help them find the way. A flashlight comes in handy at night. A few snacks can hit the spot for hungry hikers on the trail. It's important to carry a first aid kit too, in case someone is hurt or becomes sick.

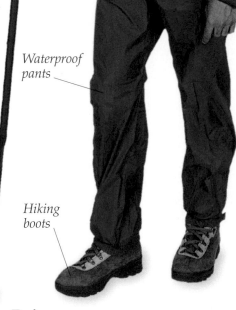

Rain parka

Waterproof pants

Hiking boots

Trail food

Small bags filled with nuts, dried fruit, granola, and other high-energy foods keep Scouts going through long days of adventure.

Flashlight

The bright beam of a flashlight shows the way after dark. A headlamp is worn on the head, which leaves the hands free.

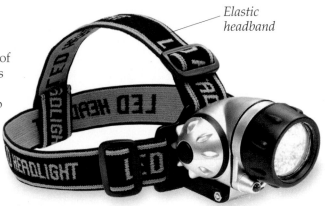

Elastic headband

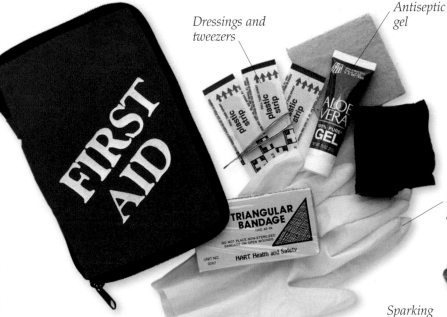

Dressings and tweezers

Antiseptic gel

Protective gloves

Rain gear

Even if there's blue sky in the morning, a storm could roll in by afternoon. Waterproof jackets and pants protect Scouts until they can reach the shelter of a tent.

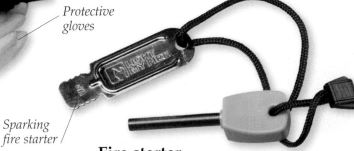

Sparking fire starter

First aid kit

A troop has a large medical kit for treating injury or illness. Each Scout also takes along a few first aid supplies in case he gets a blister or a small cut.

Fire starter

With matches or a butane lighter, Scouts can light a backpacking stove or a campfire. They keep matches and lighters dry in plastic bags.

Map and compass

Scouts can use a map and compass to figure out where they are and which way they want to go. Scouts practice navigation skills before they need to use them on a hike.

Pocketknife

It's the perfect tool for many jobs around camp. A pocketknife is easy to carry. For everything from opening cans to cutting rope, it's hard to beat.

Sun protection

Avoiding sunburn is an important health issue for everyone. Where bugs are a problem, insect repellent can be an essential, too.

Extra clothing

Layers of clothing are better than one heavy coat. Scouts can put on one layer or many depending on the weather.

Hooded jacket

Insulating layer

Warm hat

Tough backcountry pants

Water bottle

Scouts know that drinking plenty of fluids is important. Wherever they go, they always carry a water bottle.

Campouts

A PLACE WHERE PEOPLE camp outdoors is called a campsite. Scouts follow the rules of Leave No Trace to choose a spot where their camp won't harm the land. That means pitching tents away from water and not in the middle of meadows. Meals can be cooked over backpacking stoves, so that fires don't scar the ground. Scouts think of themselves as visitors in the backcountry. They know that it's important to leave an area as clean as they found it.

Campsite cooking

Scouts take turns cooking meals for their patrols. Bacon, eggs, and bread make a tasty breakfast. A pot of water heating on the stove can be used for washing the dishes.

Choosing the perfect spot

At summer camp, Scouts often sleep in big tents on beds called cots. For overnight campouts or longer expeditions, smaller tents can be better. Scouts should reach camp early enough to put up tents and cook a meal before dark.

Pitching tents

A tent for two people can be carried in a pack. To set it up, Scouts unroll the tent and slide poles into it. Thin metal stakes go through loops at the corners. The stakes are pushed into the ground to hold the tent down.

Campfire

Sitting around a fire is a big part of camping out. Scouts learn when and where to build a fire. They might roast marshmallows over the flames. It's a good time to tell stories and sing songs, too. When they want to put out the fire, they pour water over the flames. They make sure the fire is completely out before they leave camp.

Campsite Tips

✓ Always be careful with fire.

✓ Use camping stoves where fires are not allowed.

✓ Be a good neighbor to other campers.

✓ A rope tied between two trees makes a great clothesline.

✓ Store your gear inside your pack so you don't lose anything.

✓ Keep an eye on the weather and be ready to take shelter.

✓ Don't bother wild animals.

✓ Leave your camp as clean as it was when you found it.

Scout skills

ONE OF THE BEST PARTS OF SCOUTING is learning skills. First aid prepares Scouts to act in emergencies. When Scouts go camping and hiking, they need to have outdoor skills. A Scout who knows how to prepare dinner over a backpacking stove can fix meals at home, too. Cub Scouts, Boy Scouts, and Venturers practice being leaders. Learning the skills of Scouting is rewarding and fun, and it also helps all Scouts to prepare for life.

Observing wildlife

Scouting encourages boys to discover the world all around them. While they are hiking, they might see birds and other wild animals along the trail. Using a magnifying glass to watch insects in a jar is a good way to learn about them before setting them free.

Building a campfire

This Scout began building a fire with a big handful of tinder—wood shavings that will burn quickly. Above the tinder he arranged twigs called "kindling." Next he placed fuel wood in the shape of a tepee. When he lights the tinder, small flames will climb into the kindling and then catch the fuel wood on fire.

Cooking over a camping stove

In some campsites there isn't enough fuel wood to build a fire. Scouts also avoid using fires if the heat would harm plants or leave a black scar on the ground. Instead, they use camping stoves that are easy to carry and won't leave a mark on the land.

Tying a knot

Knots have thousands of uses. They are important for tying shoestrings and building a raft in camp. Scouts learn different knots for different uses. The best knots are easy to tie. They won't come undone, but they should also be easy to untie. The square knot, or Boy Scout joining knot, is the first that Scouts learn.

Understanding nature

The Earth is home to thousands of kinds of trees, shrubs, and grasses. Learning the names of plants is a good hobby. There are also guide-books for identifying birds, fish, and other animals. By understanding about plants and animals, Scouts can see how important they are for the environment.

Swimming

Knowing how to swim opens the way for plenty of fun on the water. Swimming is an important skill for safety, too. To become a Second Class Scout, a boy shows that he can swim. He also demonstrates several ways to help someone struggling in the water.

Finding the way

Practice with a map and compass gives Scouts confidence to know which way to go. If they ever get lost, they are trained to S.T.O.P. Those letters stand for Stop, Think, Observe, and Plan. Sometimes the best plan is to stay where they are and wait for others to find them.

Bobcat—First award
earned by all Cub Scouts

Tiger Cub—Age 7

Wolf—Age 8

Bear—Age 9

Webelos—Age 10

Cub Scout ranks

Every BSA program recognizes
the achievements of its
members. Cub Scouts who
complete the requirements can
wear patches showing their
ranks. Each rank is matched
Cub Scouts of a certain age.

Cub Scout ranks

THE BOY SCOUTS OF AMERICA recognizes
the accomplishments of Scouts by giving
them awards. Cub Scouts earn their way
through the ranks, from Tiger Cub through
Wolf, Bear, and Webelos. Boys can also
complete age-appropriate electives in
subjects ranging from Outdoor Adventure to
Fishing, Sports, and Computers. Tiger Cub
electives lead to the awarding of Tiger Track
Beads. Wolf and Bear Scouts are given gold
and silver arrow points. The Arrow of Light
is the highest award for Webelos Scouts.

Cub Scout earning an award

On the advancement trail, a Cub Scout progresses from
rank to rank, learning new skills as he goes. Each of
the ranks and awards in Cub Scouting has its own
requirements. They become more challenging to
match the skills learned as a Cub Scout gets older.

Cub Scout sash

Long ago, a Cub Scout's
mother sewed his awards
onto this Boy Scout merit
badge sash. He had earned
all of the rank emblems,
many arrow points, and
patches from camping trips
with his Cub Scout pack.

America's manpower begins with boypower (right)

A 1971 painting by
Norman Rockwell shows
the important role that Cub
Scouts play as members of
the Boy Scouts of America.

Merit badges

THE FIRST THREE RANKS for Boy Scouts are Tenderfoot, Second Class, and First Class. For these ranks, each Scout must pass a set of requirements. Then, they can go on to earn Star, Life, and Eagle. The requirements for these ranks include earning cloth merit badges to wear on their uniforms. They must show they have learned about a subject and practiced its skills. Today, there are more than 100 different merit badges.

Early merit badges

The first Boy Scouts could earn merit badges for Dairying, Blacksmithing, and Poultry Farming. Those badges are no longer used, but Camping, First Aid, Cooking, and Lifesaving are still around.

Log book found in caches

Route to a cache appears on GPS screen

Controls for changing GPS settings

Geocaching merit badge

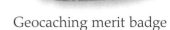

Geocaching

Geocaching is a high-tech scavenger hunt. Scouts using GPS (Global Positioning System) receivers find their way to hidden containers called caches. Inside a cache is a notebook for them to sign. There might also be trinkets for them to leave inside the next cache they find.

Cache hidden beside a soccer field

Merit badge pamphlets

Each merit badge has a pamphlet explaining the subject. The Geocaching Merit Badge pamphlet describes how to use a GPS receiver to find caches and also as a tool for Scouts traveling in the backcountry and on open water.

Merit badges

First Class Scouts must earn five merit badges to advance to the rank of Star. It takes 10 merit badges to become a Life Scout, and 21 for Eagle. Some of them are required. They include First Aid, Lifesaving, Personal Fitness, and Citizenship in the World. For the rest, Scouts can select whatever subjects they find most interesting, from American Business to Woodwork, and from Backpacking to Whitewater.

Backpacking

Chemistry

Climbing

Cooking

Crime Prevention

Cycling

Dog Care

Engineering

Fire Safety

Fishing

Nature

Nuclear Science

Public Health

Robotics

Scholarship

Space Exploration

Whitewater

Wilderness Survival

Merit badge sashes

A Scout displays his merit badges on a sash that he wears over the right shoulder of his uniform. Each Scout's sash becomes a colorful record of his achievements and a reminder of the adventure of earning merit badges.

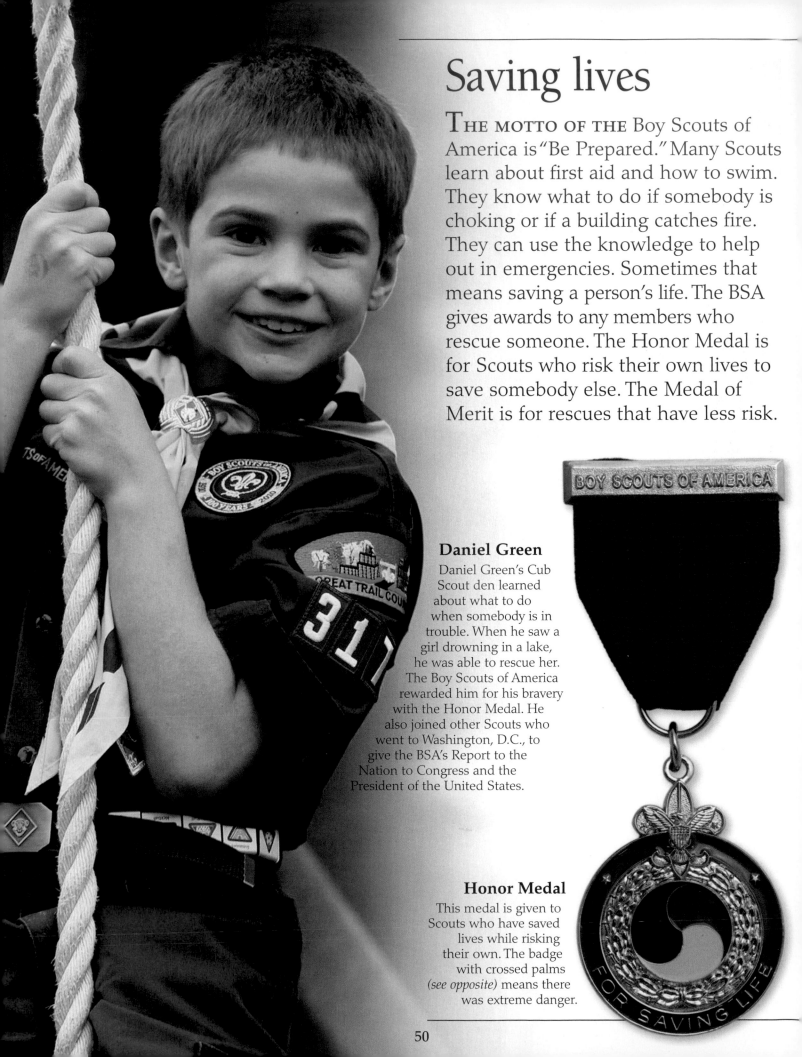

Saving lives

THE MOTTO OF THE Boy Scouts of America is "Be Prepared." Many Scouts learn about first aid and how to swim. They know what to do if somebody is choking or if a building catches fire. They can use the knowledge to help out in emergencies. Sometimes that means saving a person's life. The BSA gives awards to any members who rescue someone. The Honor Medal is for Scouts who risk their own lives to save somebody else. The Medal of Merit is for rescues that have less risk.

Daniel Green

Daniel Green's Cub Scout den learned about what to do when somebody is in trouble. When he saw a girl drowning in a lake, he was able to rescue her. The Boy Scouts of America rewarded him for his bravery with the Honor Medal. He also joined other Scouts who went to Washington, D.C., to give the BSA's Report to the Nation to Congress and the President of the United States.

Honor Medal

This medal is given to Scouts who have saved lives while risking their own. The badge with crossed palms (*see opposite*) means there was extreme danger.

A TRUE STORY OF
SCOUTS IN ACTION

He Saved His Teacher From An Oncoming Car!

Fernando Espinosa, 16, was helping a teacher cross a busy road when an oncoming car failed to stop at the crosswalk. Fernando pushed the teacher out of the way, leaving himself in the path of the approaching vehicle.

CROSS X WALK

The car hit Fernando, throwing him against the windshield and then onto the curb several feet away. The driver stopped and called 911.

Fernando suffered an injury to his left foot and was bleeding from a head wound.

Despite his injuries, Fernando rushed to check on the teacher. She had fallen, and her leg was broken in three places.

While taking deep breaths to prevent shock, Fernando put pressure on his wound using a scarf from the driver. He kept the teacher calm and assured her everything would be OK.

Paramedics arrived and tended to the teacher's injury. Fernando insisted she be taken to a hospital first. Fernando was transported in a second ambulance and received stitches to his head and knee and treatment of various scrapes and bruises.

Star Scout Fernando Espinosa, a member of Troop 4, chartered to Five Points Lions Club, El Paso, Texas, received an Honor Medal with Crossed Palms for his actions. It is Scouting's highest award for bravery.

Crossed palms

TEXT AND ART BY GRANT MIEHM

S.I.A. ON THE WEB
boyslife.org
Audio, Photos & More!

"Scouts In Action" subjects come from the National BSA Court of Honor. If you know of an act of heroism that should be recognized, contact your local BSA council office for a lifesaving or meritorious award application. Note: Consult approved safety guidelines as actions depicted here may not precisely follow standard procedures.

Boys' Life Scouts in action

Every month, *Boys' Life* magazine tells about Scouts who have saved someone's life. In every case, a Cub Scout, Boy Scout, Venturer, or leader has done his or her best. Scouting skills have been important, too. Many Scouts use what they have learned about first aid to help other people.

Honor Medal with crossed palms

Honoring America

ALL SCOUTS PROMISE TO DO their duty to their country. They learn about democracy and know that all Americans are equal. Service projects help keep their neighborhoods good places to live. Scouts understand how to report emergencies. If they see something that is wrong, they speak up. Together with other Scouts, they respect their nation by following its laws.

Citizenship in the World

Citizenship in the Nation

Citizenship

To earn the Citizenship in the World merit badge, Scouts learn how all nations are connected. To earn the Citizenship in the Nation award, boys can visit government offices and talk with public officials. To earn the Citizenship in the Community merit badge, Scouts volunteer for a charitable organization.

Citizenship in the Community

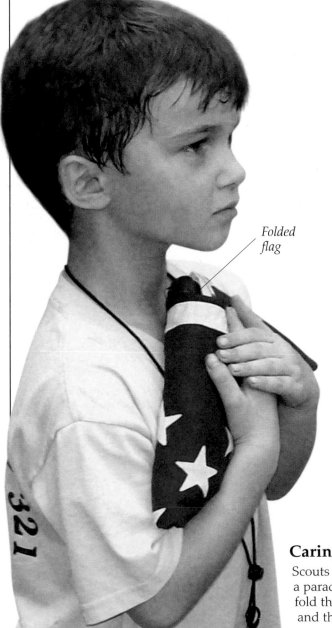

Folded flag

Color guards

Most Scout meetings begin with a flag ceremony. A color guard of Scouts raises the American flag. Everyone salutes and recites the Pledge of Allegiance. That reminds Scouts that they are part of a great nation. They also know that they have a big part to play in keeping America a country "with liberty and justice for all."

Caring for the flag

Scouts practice the right ways to display a flag in a parade, on a wall, or with other flags. They learn how to fold the American flag into a triangle with only the stars and the blue background showing. When an American flag wears out, a troop might hold a special ceremony to burn it.

Doing their best

The future of the nation is in the hands of today's young people. They can prepare themselves to be good citizens by doing their best in school. Knowledge helps us to understand other people. It also leads to careers that can help America.

Flags on parade

Scouts carry flags in parades. At a National Jamboree, there can be hundreds of flags. Scouts who see a flag going by stop whatever they are doing. They turn toward the flag. If they are wearing uniforms, they salute. People not in uniform put their right hands over their hearts.

Our nation's capital

A trip to Washington, D.C., is an exciting adventure for many Cub Scouts and Boy Scouts. They can visit the Washington Monument, the Lincoln Memorial, and the Capitol Building. Nearby are the Air and Space Museum and museums of art, history, and culture.

1937 Jamboree patch
Each Jamboree has a special patch. A Scout sews it onto his uniform to show that he attended a Jamboree. This patch is from the first Jamboree, held in 1937 in Washington, D.C.

National Jamboree

ONCE EVERY FOUR YEARS, thousands of American Scouts get together for a National Jamboree. It's a celebration of the Boy Scouts of America. Activities include everything from canoeing to riding BMX bikes. Staff at a Merit Badge Midway explain all the badges and show how to pass some of the requirements. There are also World Jamborees for Scouts from many nations. Jamborees are a great way to make friends with Scouts from all over America and around the globe.

Making camp
Troops proudly fly flags that show where they are from. With about 20,000 tents set up, the flags also help Scouts find their tents. Patrols cook breakfast and dinner in camp. Many Scouts carry sack lunches to eat during the day.

Jamboree exhibits

There is so much to do at a Jamboree, and so much to see. For example, exhibits in the Conservation Area demonstrate how Scouts can protect the environment. Scouts can also learn about many other subjects, such as wildlife, science, technology, and astronomy.

Activities

A strong harness lets Scouts fly through the trees on a cable. This zip line is part of a Jamboree problem-solving course. Scouts can do countless other sports and adventure activites, such as whitewater rafting, hiking, archery, and challenge courses.

Arena shows

Everybody attending a Jamboree gets together for several huge arena shows. Scouts enjoy music, presentations, and appearances by famous people. After dark, fireworks light up the sky.

Patch for the 2013 National Jamboree

Meet me at The Summit!

Summit Bechtel Family National Scout Reserve is the BSA's high adventure base in the rugged mountains of West Virginia. It's also home to the 2013 National Jamboree. The patch shows a Scout rappelling down a high cliff. That's just one of the Jamboree's many terrific challenges.

Boys' Life magazine

THIS MAGAZINE IS FULL OF GREAT READING for Scouts. Each month, there are stories about Boy Scouts, Cub Scouts, and Venturers having adventures. Other pages are full of puzzles, contests, and plans for things to build. Computers and video games are explained, too. Readers can learn about famous people who are interesting to boys. Pictures make everything easy to understand.

July, 1912

March, 1942

January, 2012

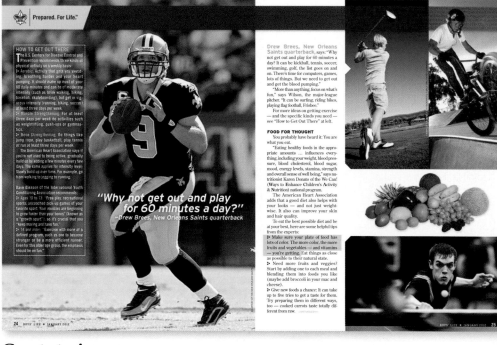

Great stories

Boys' Life stories help Scouts learn ways to stay healthy. They include exercising and eating right. Pages also explain different sports and how to play them. There are lots of ideas for camping and hiking.

Norman Rockwell

Norman Rockwell painted many pictures of Scouts. In this one, a Tenderfoot Scout is trying on his first uniform. His mother sews on patches. His brother adjusts his neckerchief. Everyone is excited about having a young Scout in the family.

Detail from Febuary, 1958 cover

36   BOYS' LIFE ✦ JANUARY 2012

Pee Wee Harris

There are lots of cartoons in *Boys' Life* magazine. The star of one of them is Pee Wee Harris. He and his friends find plenty of excitement with their troop.

Pedro

Pedro is the *Boys' Life* mascot. He delivers the mail to the *Boys' Life* office, and every month he has funny things to say. He signs his name with his hoof prints like this—UU.

Pee Wee Harris cartoon from January, 2012

Think and Grin

The last page is called Think and Grin. It is full of jokes that boys have sent to *Boys' Life*. Here's one:
Question: "Why are elephants big and gray?"
Answer: "Because if they were small and purple they would be grapes."

100th anniversary edition

Famous Scouts

EXPLORERS

Neil Armstrong

The first man to walk on the Moon was Eagle Scout Neil Armstrong. As he looked into the lunar sky, he could see the planet Earth almost 239,000 miles away. The round-trip flight to the Moon took about nine days.

Steve Fossett

The record for flying a balloon non-stop around the world was set by Steve Fossett. As a pilot, mountain climber, and sailor he led a life full of adventure. He was a successful businessman, too, and an Eagle Scout.

Paul Siple

When Eagle Scout Paul Siple was just 19, he went to Antarctica on an expedition with a famous explorer named Richard Byrd. Paul spent the rest of his life as an expert on the South Pole and living in very cold places.

Jim Whittaker

Star Scout Jim Whittaker was the first American to climb to the top of Mount Everest, the highest mountain in the world. The summit of Everest is as high as cruising altitude for airliners. The air was so thin that Jim had to breathe oxygen through a mask.

POLITICAL LEADERS

Michael Bloomberg

The mayor of New York City is an Eagle Scout who became one of the richest people in the world. He is also a philanthropist—someone who gives money to causes he feels are worthwhile.

Stephen Breyer

Eagle Scout Breyer is one of nine justices on the Supreme Court, the highest court in the United States. The court meets in Washington, D.C., to decide on legal cases that are important to people all over America.

Gerald Ford

The 38th president of the United States learned some of his leadership skills while earning the Eagle Scout Award. He played football at the University of Michigan on a team that won two national championships.

Gary Locke

The first Chinese-American to be governor of a state was Eagle Scout Gary Locke from Seattle, Washington. President Obama named him U.S. ambassador to China. He helps America and China figure out ways to work together for the good of both countries.

SCIENTISTS AND BUSINESSMEN

William C. DeVries

Doctor William C. DeVries, an Eagle Scout, was the first surgeon to replace the heart of a sick person with an artificial heart. The mechanical device pumped blood just like a real heart. Thanks to Dr. DeVries' research, many people are alive today because they have artificial hearts.

Bill Gates

Life Scout Bill Gates used to show others in his troop how computers worked. He learned all he could about computer programming, then went on to build a giant software company called Microsoft.

Rex Tillerson

The oil and gas company ExxonMobil is one of the biggest businesses in the world. It is led by Eagle Scout Rex Tillerson. As a volunteer, he also served as President of the Boy Scouts of America.

Sam Walton

When he was a young man, Sam opened a little store called Walton's. The lessons the Eagle Scout learned there helped him start Walmart and make it grow. Today, Walmart has more than 10,000 stores in 27 nations.

Neil Armstrong

Gary Locke

Harrison Ford

The star of the *Indiana Jones* movies was a Life Scout. In the movies, so was his character, Indiana Jones. Harrison Ford also played the part of Han Solo in *Star Wars*. A star with his name is on a sidewalk called the Hollywood Walk of Fame.

Wynton Marsalis

This Eagle Scout grew up in a Louisiana family with brothers and a father who were all jazz musicians. Wynton learned to play the trumpet. The recordings he has made have won awards around the world. He plays many concerts and shares his music by teaching others.

Mike Rowe

The host of the television show *Dirty Jobs* has fun exploring work where people get dirty. At the 2010 National Jamboree, Mike Rowe, an Eagle, gave a speech to 45,000 Scouts. He likes to say that everything he knows he learned as a Boy Scout.

Jimmy Stewart

As a boy, Jimmy Stewart was a Second Class Scout. As an adult, he starred in many movies, including *It's a Wonderful Life*. This film is shown on television almost every Christmas. For his support of young people, he received the Silver Buffalo Award from the Boy Scouts of America.

Hank Aaron

Eagle Scout "Hammerin' Hank" Aaron stands tall as one of America's greatest professional baseball players. He played for many years on teams in Milwaukee and Atlanta. His record of 755 home runs was not broken for more than 30 years.

Willie Banks

This athlete and Eagle Scout represented the U.S. in three different Olympic games. He set the world record of almost 60 feet for the triple jump—a hop, skip, and jump into a sand pit.

Bill Bradley

A top student and athlete at Princeton University, Bill Bradley went on to play basketball for the New York Knicks. The Eagle Scout served in Congress as a senator representing New Jersey. In 2000, he ran for president of the United States.

Mark Spitz

At the 1972 Olympics, swimmer and former Cub Scout Mark Spitz won seven gold medals. His races included the butterfly, freestyle, and relays. At that time, no athlete had ever won so many gold medals at one Olympics.

Mike Rowe

Willie Banks

Questions and answers

Q Has a Scout ever earned all the merit badges?

A Some have, but not many. It takes lots of work to earn the 21 badges needed to become an Eagle Scout. Adding a hundred more is a real challenge.

Eagle Scout

Q Can girls be Boy Scouts?

A No, but they can be Venturers. Venturing is the Boy Scouts of America's youth development program for young men and women who want to enjoy fantastic Scouting adventures together.

Venturers

Q Are any places named for Boy Scouts?

A Yes, some mountains are. Eagle Scout Peak and Mount Baden-Powell are in California. Mount Ernest Thompson Seton in Montana and Mount Dan Beard in Alaska honor two other founders of Scouting.

Mount Dan Beard

Q What is the Order of the Arrow, or OA?

A It's the BSA's national honor society. Members are elected by other Scouts. The OA develops leadership skills and encourages older boys to stay involved in Scouting.

Order of the Arrow

Eagle Scout Phil Smart, Sr.

Q Who is the oldest Eagle Scout?

A No one knows for sure. Many men over 90 years old are proud to show off the Eagle Scout pins they earned a long time ago. One of them is Phil Smart, Sr.

Q Are there Boy Scouts in other nations?

A There are more than 30 million Scouts in 161 countries. Each nation's Scouts have their own uniforms, badges, and programs.

Scout from South Africa

Questions and answers

Q What are World Jamborees?

A Every four years Scouts from around the globe travel to a host country to camp together. Activities at a World Jamboree encourage Scouts to form friendships that can last a lifetime.

Flags at a World Jamboree parade

Q Was Walt Disney ever a Boy Scout?

A For a short time. As an adult he was a big supporter of Scouting. The Walt Disney Pictures movie *Follow Me Boys* shows the adventures of a Scoutmaster leading a troop.

Walt Disney

Lone Scout patch

Q Can a boy be a Scout if there is not a troop nearby?

A As a Lone Scout he can take part in BSA programs on his own. Responsible adults in his life will help him make the most of the experience.

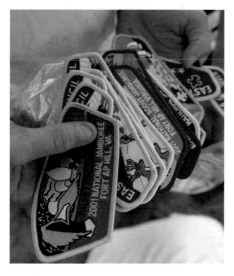

Patch trading

Q What is "patch trading"?

A Scouts attending National Jamborees get to meet boys from all over America. Exchanging patches from local councils is a way that Scouts can seal new friendships.

Q Where is the National Headquarters of the BSA?

A It is in Irving, Texas, near the Dallas-Fort Worth Airport. Next door is the National Scouting Museum. It's a great place to visit to learn about Scouting's history.

BSA National Headquarters

Q Why did early Scouts wear hats with broad brims?

A Robert Baden-Powell, the founder of Scouting, liked this style of hat. Boys found it protected them from sun and rain. Some Scouts today still wear hats like this.

Early hat

Fascinating facts

■ The William T. Hornaday Award is Scouting's "Olympic medal" for outstanding efforts in environmental conservation.

■ Of 541 Senators and Congressmen in the 112th Congress of the United States, 208 have been Boy Scouts or adult leaders, and 29 have been Eagle Scouts.

■ The National Scouting Museum in Irving, Texas, has more than half a million items telling the history of the Boy Scouts of America. They include the first Eagle Scout pin and the latest Boy Scout Handbook.

■ Scouts share knot-tying and other skills with each other using the Teaching EDGE—Explain, Demonstrate, Guide, and Enable.

■ Ernest Thompson Seton, one of the founders of the BSA was so interested in wolves that he called himself Black Wolf and drew a wolf footprint next to his signature.

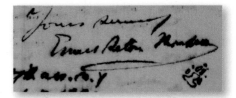

■ In 1980, the Boy Scouts wanted a new look for the uniform. Famous fashion designer Oscar de la Renta came up with a tan shirt and olive green pants.

■ Scouts have earned more than 110 million merit badges. The most popular are First Aid, Swimming, and Camping.

■ One in three cadets at the U.S. Army and Air Force military academies was a Boy Scout. So was one in four Naval Academy midshipmen.

■ President Theodore Roosevelt believed so much in the BSA that he was named First Scout Citizen.

■ Project COPE stands for Challenging Outdoor Personal Experience. Obstacle courses and zip lines encourage teamwork and problem solving.

■ During his term in office, every U.S. president is also the honorary president of the BSA.

■ Early Scouts used flags to send messages with Morse code or semaphore.

■ Twelve men have walked on the Moon. Eleven of them have been Boy Scouts.

■ Boy Scout pocketknives are almost the same today as they were a hundred years ago. Tents, stoves, and other outdoor equipment have changed a lot.

■ Philmont Scout Ranch in New Mexico was given to the Boy Scouts by a businessman named Waite Phillips. The word "Philmont" combines part of his last name with part of the word "mountain."

Glossary

BASIC ESSENTIALS Ten items that Scouts carry with them when hiking and camping. The pocketknife, rain gear, and other items can come in handy along the way.

CACHE A small container that is the goal of a scavenger hunt for Scouts using GPS receivers.

CAMPOUT An overnight trip by Scouts to sleep in tents, cook meals in the open, and enjoy the outdoors.

COLOR GUARD A group of Scouts who carry the American flag during ceremonies at troop meetings or other special events.

COURT OF HONOR A special ceremony held to present Boy Scouts with awards they have earned.

CUB SCOUT DEN Six to eight boys within a Cub pack who meet several times a month between pack meetings.

CUB SCOUT MOTTO The Cub Scout Motto is "Do Your Best." Cub Scouts learn that if they do the best they can at everything, then no one can find fault with them.

CUB SCOUT PACK A group of all the Cub Scout dens that gets together monthly.

EAGLE SCOUT AWARD The highest rank earned by Boy Scouts. Requirements include being a troop leader and earning 21 merit badges.

GPS RECEIVER An electronic compass and route-finding device Scouts use to find their way. The letters GPS stand for Global Positioning System.

GOOD TURN The Scout promise to do something for others every day without asking for payment.

NATIONAL JAMBOREE A national gathering of thousands of Scouts to celebrate Scouting. The National Scout Jamboree takes place every four years. Its new home is the Summit Bechtel Family National Scout Reserve (The Summit) in West Virginia. World Scout Jamborees bring together Scouts from many nations.

LEAVE NO TRACE Guidelines that Scouts use to protect the land while they are hiking and camping.

MERIT BADGES Awards earned by Boy Scouts for completing requirements in more than 100 subjects including First Aid, Music, Robotics, and Inventing.

NATIONAL HIGH ADVENTURE BASES Four BSA areas that offer outdoor experiences for older Scouts. The bases are located at Philmont Scout Ranch in New Mexico, Florida Sea Base, Northern Tier in Minnesota and Canada, and the Summit Bechtel Reserve™ in West Virginia.

NECKERCHIEF A colorful cloth that Scouts in uniform can wear around their necks.

PINEWOOD DERBY RACER A gravity-propelled wooden car built by a Cub Scout with his parent/guardian.

PLEDGE OF ALLEGIANCE A promise to show respect for the U.S.

RANKS Levels of achievement for Scouts. Cub Scout ranks are Tiger Cub, Wolf, Bear, and Webelos. Boy Scout ranks are Tenderfoot, Second Class, First Class, Star, Life, and Eagle. Awards for Venturers are Bronze, Gold, and Silver, Ranger, Quest, TRUST, and the Venturing Leadership Award.

SCOUT LAW A set of 12 guidelines for life that Boy Scouts repeat at the beginning of troop meetings and during some other BSA events while they make the Scout Sign.

SCOUT OATH A promise that Scouts make to be good Scouts and good citizens. They make the Scout sign when they say the Scout Oath.

SCOUT SALUTE Made by forming the Scout sign and touching the hand to the forehead. The salute is used to honor the American flag.

SCOUT SIGN Raising the right hand and extending two fingers (for Cub Scouts) or three fingers (for Boy Scouts). The sign is made while reciting the Cub Scout Promise and the Boy Scout Oath and Law.

SEMAPHORE A way of sending messages using flags. The flags are held in different positions for each letter.

SENIOR PATROL LEADER The highest-ranking youth leader of a Boy Scout troop.

SLEEPING BAG Insulated bedding that a Scout can unroll in his tent for a warm night's sleep.

SQUARE KNOT The first knot that Boy Scouts learn how to tie. It is also called the joining knot.

TROOP A unit of Scouts that usually meets once a week. It is made up of patrols, groups of six to eight Boy Scouts.

UNIFORM The clothing worn by Scouts. Looking alike shows that all Scouts are equal.

VENTURING The young adult program of the BSA for men and women ages 14 through 20, or 13 with completion of the eighth grade.

ZIP LINE A cable attached between two trees or poles that Scouts can slide along while attached by a harness.

Index

AB

Aaron, Hank 59
adventures 7, 14–15, 36–37, 38–39
Akela 9
arena shows 55
Armstrong, Neil 58
Arrow of Light Award 18, 30, 46
awards 7, 46–47, 48–49, 52
axes 15
Baden-Powell, Robert 8–9, 10, 60, 61
badges 12, 25, 46, 48–49, 60, 62, 63
Banks, Willie 59
basic essentials 40–41, 63
Bear rank 46
Beard, Daniel Carter 10, 11, 60
Birch Bark Roll, The 10
Black Wolf 10, 62
Bloomberg, Michael 58
blueprints, Pinewood Derby® cars 22
boats 39
Bobcat 46
Boer War 8
Boone, Daniel 11
Boy Scout Handbook, The 16–17
Boyce, William 26
Boys' Life magazine 51, 56–57
Bradley, Bill 59
Breyer, Stephen 58
Britain 8–9

CD

caches 48, 63
campfires 18, 30, 43, 44
camps 14, 20
  campouts 32, 42–43, 63
  National Jamborees 54
  Silver Bay 14–15
  summer camps 34
  winter camping 39
canoe trips 37, 39
cars, Pinewood Derby® 20, 21, 22–23
cartoons 57
citizenship awards 52
clothing 12–13, 40, 41, 62, 63
color guards 52, 63
community help 21, 26, 28–29
compasses 35, 41, 45
Congress 62
Conservation Area 55
cooking 42, 44
COPE, Project 62
cots 42
Cub Scouts 9, 18–19, 20–21, 46–47
  awards 18, 30, 46
  Law of the Pack, The 9
  meetings 20–21
  motto 25, 50, 63
  Oath 25
  Promise 25
  packs 18, 63
  ranks 19, 46, 63
  salute 20
  sign 20, 24
cycling 33
Daniel Green 50
de la Renta, Oscar 62
Den Chief 20, 21
den leaders 20, 21
dens, Cub Scout 18, 19, 20, 21, 18, 63
DeVries, William C. 58
disabled Scouts 32
Disney, Walt 61
diving 37, 39

EFG

Eagle Scout 7, 48, 49, 60, 63
Eagle Scout Peak, California 60
electives, Cub Scout 46
emergencies 50
England *see* United Kingdom
environment 27, 28
equipment 40–41
expeditions 36
field trips 20
fire starters 40
fires 30, 43, 44
first aid 50–51
first aid kits 14, 40
First Class Scouts 49
fishing 34
flags 52–3
  semaphore 16, 64
flashlights 40
Florida Sea Base 37
food 27, 40, 42
Ford, Gerald 58
Ford, Harrison 59
Fossett, Steve 58
friendship 6, 19
games 20
Gates, Bill 58
geocaching 48
girls 40
Good Turns 6, 9, 26–27, 63
GPS (Global Positioning System) 35, 48, 63
graffiti, removing 29

HIJ

Harris, Pee Wee 57
hats 9, 12, 61
high adventures 36–37
hikemeters 15
hiking 18, 20, 35, 40
Honor Medal 50, 51
honor societies 60
honoring America 25, 31, 52–3
horseback riding 33
Irving, Texas 61
Jamboree 53, 54–55, 61, 63
Jungle Book, The 9

KL

Kipling, Rudyard 9
knives 14, 41, 62
knots 45, 63
Law of the Pack, The 9
Law 9, 16, 24, 63
League of Woodcraft Indians 10
learning 7, 18
Leave No Trace rule 42, 29, 63
life saving 50–51
Life Scout 46, 49

MNO

Mafeking 8, 9
magazine, *Boys' Life* 51, 56–57
maps 41, 45
Marsalis, Wynton 59
mascot, *Boys' Life* magazine 57
Medal of Merit 50
medals 23, 28, 50, 51
meetings 31
merit badges 12, 48–49, 60, 62, 63
Moon 58, 62
mottoes 16, 24, 25, 50, 63
Mount Baden-Powell, California 60
Mount Dan Beard, Alaska 60
Mount Ernest Thompson Seton, Montana 60
mountaineering 38
National Headquarters 61
National High Adventure Bases 37, 63
National Jamboree 53, 54–55, 61, 63
National Scouting Museum, Irving, Texas 61, 62
Naval Academy 62
navigation 35, 41, 45
neckerchief slides 13
neckerchiefs 13, 30, 63
Nelson, Lloyd 14
Northern Tier 37
oath 16, 20, 24, 28, 63
Order of the Arrow 60

PQR

packs, Trapper Nelson 14
packs, Cub Scout 18, 63
pamphlets, merit badge 48
patch trading 61
patches 12, 13, 18, 46, 54
patrol leaders 31
patrols 30, 63
Lobo 10
Locke, Gary 58
Lone Scouts 61
Pedro 57
Pee Wee Harris 57
Phillips, Waite 62
Philmont Scout Ranch 37, 62
Pinewood Derby® 20, 21, 22–23, 63
Pledge of Allegiance 20, 52, 63
pocketknives 14, 41, 62
Promise, Cub Scout 25
presidents, U.S. 62
Project COPE 62
rain gear 40
ranks 18, 19, 46, 63
rappelling 32, 38
religion 25
Report to the Nation 44
Rockwell, Norman 46, 56
Roosevelt, Theodore 62
Rowe, Mike 59

STUV

sailing 39
salute 24, 16, 53, 63
sashes, merit badge 46, 49
saving lives 50–51
Scout Law 9, 24, 16, 63
Scout Oath 16, 24, 28, 63
Scout sign 24, 16, 63
Scouting for Boys (Baden-Powell) 8, 9
"Scouting for Food" 27
Scoutmasters 31
Scuba diving 37, 39
Sea Scouts 16, 39
Second Class Scouts 48
semaphore 16, 62
senior patrol leaders 31, 63
Seton, Ernest Thompson 10, 60, 62
ships 39
sign, Cub Scout 20
Silver Bay, New York State 14
Siple, Paul 58
skills 30, 44–45
sleeping bags 32, 63
slides, neckerchief 13
slogan 25, 16
Smart, Phil, Sr. 60
Sons of Daniel Boone 11
Spitz, Mark 59

WXYZ

Walton, Sam 58
Washington, D.C. 53
water bottles 41
water sports 34, 39
Webelos 18, 25, 46
West, James E. 10, 11
whistles 15
Whittaker, Jim 58
wildlife 34, 44, 45
William T. Hornaday Award 62
winter camping 39
Wolf rank 10, 34, 46
wolves 10, 62
Woodcraft League of America 10
World Jamboree 54, 61, 63

sports programs 18
square knot 45, 63
Star Scout 48
stargazing 33
Stewart, Jimmy 59
stoves 42, 44
summer camps 34
Summit Bechtel Family National Scout Reserve 55, 63
sun protection 41
swimming 34, 45
teamwork 6, 19
Tenderfoot Scouts 48, 56
tents 42, 54
Think and Grin 57
Tiger Cubs 19, 46
Tillerson, Rex 58
trail food 40
Trapper Nelson pack 14
Treasury medal 28
troops 30–31, 63
uniforms 9, 12–13, 62, 63
United Kingdom 8–9
U.S. Air Force cadets 62
U.S. Army cadets 62
U.S. Congress 62
U.S. presidents 62
values 20, 24–25
Venturing 48–49, 60, 63
Venturers 6, 38–39, 44, 60, 63

Acknowledgments

Dorling Kindersley would like to thank **Christy Batchelor** for supplying photographs from the Boys Scouts of America image library.

The publisher would also like to thank the following for their kind permission to reproduce their photographs:

(Key: a-above; b-below/bottom; c-center; f-far; l-left; r-right; t-top)

5 Brown and Bigelow, Inc.: Joseph Csatari / and with permission of the Boy Scouts of America. Printed under license from the Boy Scouts of America. (tr). **6 Corbis:** Ana Venegas / The Orange County Register / ZUMA Press (tl). **8 Getty Images:** Mansell / Time & Life Pictures (tl). **22 Alamy Images:** Ted Foxx (tl). **23 Alamy Images:** Ken Stewart / ZUMA Press / ZUMA Wire Service (b).

24 Boy Scouts of America: Joseph Csatari (tl). **47 Brown and Bigelow, Inc.:** Norman Rockwell / and with permission of the Boy Scouts of America. **50 Akron Beacon Journal:** (l). **56 Brown and Bigelow, Inc.:** Norman Rockwell / and with permission of the Boy Scouts of America (br). **58 Corbis:** Imaginechina (br). **Getty Images:** AFP / NASA (bl). **59 Getty Images:** Bob Thomas Sports Photography (r); Frederick M. Brown (bl). **60 Alamy Images:** Daniel H. Bailey / Alaska Stock (c). **61 Corbis:** Bettmann (bl). **62 Corbis:** Jay M. Pasachoff / Science Faction (tr).

Jacket images: *Front*: **Courtesy of the Boy Scouts of America:** Randy Piland (main image).

All other images courtesy of the Boy Scouts of America.

About the author

Eagle Scout Robert Birkby is author of the current editions of *The Boy Scout Handbook* and *Fieldbook*. As a college student, he worked six summers at Philmont Scout Ranch repairing and building trails in the backcountry. Now a writer, photographer, and adventure travel guide, he is deeply involved with conservation efforts around the world.